Organic Matters

Anna Asquith

Presentation by *BookLeaf Publishing*

Web: www.bookleafpub.com

E-mail: info@bookleafpub.com

ISBN: 9789357619844

First edition 2022

*To my loving husband and beautiful boys - who
constantly push me to be better.*

ACKNOWLEDGEMENT

Thanks to Timeka - for inspiring the title and encouraging me to continue this process.

PREFACE

This is entirely new to me. I have always been fond of words and the comfort they offer when processing thoughts and emotions. This book aspires not to be great. Just to share some imagery and light to random thoughts that some may or may not connect with.

Island

Missing fit.
One side not matching the other.
Square peg, round hole.
Walking. Dazed.
Waiting. Hoping. Yearning.
A small island. Isolated.
Isolated island.
Many more around.
Just none connected.
The child awaits. Yearning to feel whole.
Basking in the sound of lapping waves.
Breathe in - breathe out.
We'll rest here a little longer.

Blip

Just a bite-sized chunk,
of text to capture a moment.
One moment in time,
clicking away.
Sometimes slow....
Sometimes not.
Sometimes meaningful,
Sometimes not.
Sometimes you catch it and feel it,
Yet those moments are rare.
Most of the time,
Time just ticks. On. By.

Mirror

Light filters through the seemingly insignificant
gaps
Almost impossible to see via the naked eye
Tangled among the humour and self-sabotage
I still see you.
Spark, laughter, talent.
Sabotage.
But then a glimmer sparkles,
An illumination….
The door slams.
Cracks creep.
Yet, they can still seal.
And heal.
With time and trust.
The noise can be deafening.
The road is long.
When I see you, I see me.

Rant

Hey there mister, shouting at me,
I don't think you realise how aggressive you
seem.
If I delve below the surface, I'm sure there's
pain,
But this manifests as you needing something to
gain.

Hey there man, shouting at us,
we're heading out for dinner, not expecting this
fuss.
You can take your paper, and put it away,
We don't hear a single word you say.

Hey there sir, I feel for you,
If shouting at 'non believing' people, is what you
need to do.
I'm merely a human, here on this Earth,
Doing human things, with ideas to birth,

I may not be, just like you,
But I am here, to do great things too.

Safe

Feeling good,
It's a new kind of feeling.
To feel supported,
And somewhat reborn.
Something so tiny,
Flows through the bloodstream.
Renewing my cells,
Rewiring my mind.
What took me so long?
To ignore the stigma.
My brain just needed to be held,
To calmly transform.

Moments

6

Six and full of sunshine,
I ruffle my fingers through your hair.
One last tickle, one last cuddle,
I'll tuck you in with your teddy bear.
You're a bucket full of sweetness,
My heart may just burst.
Growing up so quickly,
Time can feel like a curse.
My pocket full of sunshine,
I can feel that little heart beating.
I can't believe it's been six years,
The moments are fleeting.
Don't grow up too quickly,
Or wish your life away.
You're counting down til you turn seven,
Rest my darling, just lay.

Positive

Just 'think positive!'
Screw that.
Stupid sentiment.
Thoughts come and thoughts go,
Feelings come and feelings go.
The more we push them down,
The harder they'll fight.
They'll show up and project,
Their ugly heads.
The harshest, ugliest,
Versions of themselves
And that's what people will remember.
The outburst.
The coloured transmission,
Of all that has been buried,
And bubbling below the surface,
for so long.
So no, I won't think or feel 'positive'
I choose to embrace what I think and feel,
Right at this very moment.

Light

8

Mr Sensitive,
Gosh I love your heart.
I may not show it sometimes,
But it's tricky.
You and I are so similar,
so it can be somewhat confronting.
Like a slap in the face,
Or a slammed door.
I will let my guard down,
I know how much we need each other.
To learn side by side.
Embrace who you are, my love.
You'll find your people.
It's OK to bear all the emotions you do,
The world needs your light.

Fluid

Ebbs and flows,
One day to the next.
Different to yesterday.
Floating,
Flowing.
I am,
I am.
Unfixed,
Fluid.
A web of experiences,
That shape.
Not defined,
By this human form.
I am more.
Changing.
Evolving.
A human,
Being.

Destruction

Oh the fire, it burns so bright,
Destroying all in its line of sight.
Always ready to pick a fight,
Even when calm, you can see its light.
A flicker of a flame, a lick of a tongue,
If you approach, you may regret you've come.
It will easily scare off some,
Though the ones that battle are the worthy ones.

Phoenix

Can you see it?
That glimpse of brightness,
That still exists,
Deep within you.
I know that sometimes, it may feel muted,
Depleted – or even gone.
I promise you, it's still there.
I see it.
Under the rubble, dirt and layers,
The pure essence of you is still there.
You will not be buried by the layers.
I know you will rise.
And reflect,
On that shadow you emerged from.
As this is just the shedding,
Of an old part of you.
You'll stand in your power,
As one in a million.

Unravelling

A single loose thread,
Suddenly caught.
The spiral begins.
Round and around.
Few rows gone.
The speed picks up.
Boldly and bravely,
A knot appears.
Clutching on tightly,
The intricate complexities,
are harder to release.
Faster, faster,
With greater force.
Until the former shape,
Is no longer recognisable.
A tangled pile lies on the floor,
With hope to be shaped into something new,
Someday.

Steam Roller

Steam roller.
Rolling over.
Old paths.
Cycle breaker.
Circuit shaker.
Generation hijacker,
For those to come.
Tiny increments,
Small adjustments.
Adding up,
To definitive change.

Ocean

14

Push - pull,
Take me with you.
Drag me under,
Immerse me in your calm.
Roll me around,
Weightless. Care-less.
Return me home,
Somewhat renewed.
Stay, don't leave me,
Keep me protected.
You free my mind,
Body and soul.

Shhh!

Shhh!
I hear what you're saying,
I need you to stop.
I know what you're doing,
You're playing 'bad cop'.
You're trying to squash,
The goodness I'm feeling.
I'm trying to ignore you,
I'm working through healing.
I'm tired of the record,
Circling round, round, round.
I close my eyes and exhale,
It's fading, for now.

Bound

I look at our hands.
They look so different now,
From when we began.
Time has made its mark on us.
I feel your grasp so tight,
Yet sometimes, I hardly feel your grip at all.
For so many reasons,
on your side and mine.
We are bound in this lifetime,
Despite occasional resistance.
Though, I may not always show it.
You're strength carries me through.
I'm forever grateful.

Ignoramus

Blinkers on.
Eyes shut.
Oh how I envy thee!
To be able to turn off
The ability to worry
Or even care
About occurs outside
Of your immediate bubble.
Yet, I still care for you.
And your pain.
Having a heart
That experiences the biggest of feelings
Can truly be a lot to bear at times.
A blessing and a curse
I feel your detachment and numbness
The pain you cannot afford to feel

Connect

Hello there,
How are you?
You'll tell me you're fine,
It's what you're trained to say.
But,
How are you?
Really?
Tell me what's on your heart,
In your soul.
I have time.
You're not alone.
If you don't want to talk,
Let's just sit.
Here is a place,
Any place will do.
It's OK,
To not be fine.
I'm here,
For you.
Whenever you need.

Breakaway

One foot in,
One on the shore.
A finger testing the temperature,
Sensing the intrigue.
To be swept forward,
Thrusted into the unknown.
Yet my net,
Wants to keep me safe.
It prevents the potential mistake,
That putting yourself in the open water can
enable.
Yet, if I don't take the chance,
I will never know.
So I shall jump,
Create that splash.
Carrying those memories from before,
Close to my heart.

www.ingramcontent.com/pod-product-compliance
Lightning Source LLC
La Vergne TN
LVHW050302200726
843509LV00015B/3118